Never Trust Where a Cat Sits

Irene A. Mosvold

SOUTHWORD *editions*

First published in 2005
by Southword Editions
The Munster Literature Centre
Frank O'Connor House, 84 Douglas Street,
Cotk, Ireland.
www.munsterlit.ie

Set in Centaur
Printed by Colour Books, Dublin.

Cover Image: Self Portrait 1997 by Debbie Dawson Stained Glass
Back Cover Image: Self Portrait 1996 by Debbie Dawson Etched and Painted Glass.

Acknowledgements

'The Right Time to Die' was third in the Scriobh Poetry Competition.

Contents

For
Peter, Sally and Sridhar, Gillian, Alexis and Erik

Give It Up for Lent

Give me a pussified man
any day of the week
I'll fry him up
he'll smell so sweet
I'll slice him
and serve him on wheaten toast
a testosterone cocktail
for my next gracious host.

He'll fit in the freezer just fine
easier than he'll fit in me
at least then he'll be all mine
and I'll know where he'll be.

It really is a shame,
macho men taste so much better all the way round.
By the time I'm done
I'll have solved the homeless problem in this town.

Siting the House

Never trust where a cat sits, for she will always pick the wrong
spot,
a space where you won't fit.

But the dog's instincts, if left intact, if not interfered with, will
always hold true.
Watch where they sit and you will know where comfort lies.

The cat will sit where the rattlers sun and twitch her tail across
warm granite.

The dog will circle and sit and inspect; he will move away from
underground streams,
past places pleasant to the eye, until he is satisfied with how the
ground feels.
Then he will sit; where he lies you build your house.

Barometer

He listened to the weather forecast: considerable miserableness
with periods of depression and suicidal despair. Brief
intermittent showers. Short squalls of rage possible,
accompanied by low westerly winds. Heavy precipitation
in the evening.

It was always this way, he thought, flicking off the channel.
It was always this way on the dark side of the year.

Nice Feet

Take those farmer's feet of yours
and walk all over me
find the wet spots
and those you've ignored
for years, left overgrown
untrimmed.

Dig your heel in my packed clay
where water pools in great lakes
scrape your horny toenails
across the surface of my spring lake.

Please yourself in my furrowed fields
rows lined up and stippled
like so much iron muscle
hold my earth in your hand
then turn me over
do it all again.

Sing a song of sick men
pockets full of lye
four and twenty blackbirds
caked upon my thigh.
When my skin was washed off
the birds
began to walk
they pulled the pennies from my eyes
and I began to talk:

My husband's with his law clerk
on his hands and knees,
his mistress in the powder room
counting up her fees,
their bastard's in the army
polishing his nose,
down comes my blackbird
and pecks off his hose.

Good to the Last Drop

They always come back for more
even thirty years later
here he is, knocking at my door
I'll let him in, sure I will
hand him a glass of gin
wait 'till he's good and soused
push him to the bedroom
and squeeze every last drop of liquor
out of him.

The Right Time to Die
for Werner Herzog

A message arrived: Come quickly, it said. She is dying.

I could keep her alive if I walked from Munich to Paris

my needy feet pinning her soul in place.

I took the straightest route, through fields and hills.

If my feet were on the ground she would be too, but
if I took the train or a plane she would vanish
like the quickflash of a photographer's bulb.

The winter was bitter. I walked.

She recovered by the time I arrived, and went on to live nine
                                        more years.

One day, in her nineties, she looked at me over lunch and said,
                            "Leben sott, I am done.
But I cannot leave. I feel there is a spell on me, keeping me
                                        here."

Lotte, I said, there is no spell upon you.

Two weeks later she was dead.

A Really good Day and How to Tell if You're Having One

A really good day
begins when a friend asks –
publicly – 'Haven't you
been through menopause yet??'
and you stick out your tongue,
                    say no
and steal her boyfriend.
That's a really good day.

When she asks 'Why not?'
you say you have bypassed menopause
and gone straight to juvenile
delinquency, and in fact,
you rather like it that way.
Then you steal her husband.
That's a really good day.

When she remarks, 'Really??
Are you sure??' in a high
squeaky voice,
you can nod
with all the wisdom of your years.

Then you realize she's gay.

Who Cares What You Need?

What you want
won't walk in your front door
you want the man who delivers
no matter the season or hour.

You want an outdoor man
one who's used to the cold
used to having to warm himself up
with very little to hold.

You want one who can get the job done
without a lot of fuss or noise
who won't attract the neighbours' attention
when he pins you to the wall joists.

One who can hoist you off your feet
and cook you dinner afterwards
clean up the mess he's made
keep his mouth shut, and keep his word.

My Son the Lynx

Changeling child,
who smiles up at me, incisors just starting to protrude.
His sisters object to his extra teeth
but then they only see him as human.
I know his feral nature
his grey fur, his tipped tawny ears, his sleekness, his
                                  secretiveness.

I have taught him not to sniff people.
It's rude, can't do that.
Must use your other senses;
keep your cat nature hid.
Just because, I explain.
That's how it is when you live here.

I put off the dentist;
I know if I have those two teeth pulled
he will not be able to change back.
Then he will lift his nose to the wind
and remember
what he was
before.

When
the phone doesn't ring
that's me
thinking of you.

When the mailbox is empty
that's me
writing you.

When you see something move
out of the corner of your eye
that's me
watching you.

When your heart sinks to your feet
that's me
pulling you.

When the hair on your neck rises
that's me
stalking you.

When you can't breathe
that's me
choking you.

He watched as she slept
her arms and legs akimbo
like an origami swan
loosing its folds.

Ariadneae

O to be a spider
and collect my pinprick
of delight;

Brainmeal entrée
with booklungs on the side.

Diaxial fangs follow
amorous pursuits.

Don't Count On It

Don't count on my good nature
I still might run you over with the car
or truck or whatever farm implement
comes to hand. Misery loves company
that's why I love you.

Don't count on good intentions
I haven't very many left;
most were squeezed out of me
last lifetime around and this time
I have to be sparing.

So you can hang out here
if you don't take up too much space
don't make too many demands
none at all is best. You can stay
if you leave me the hell alone.

Dear Herpetic Eruption,

You can't be serious about going out and finding

someone tonight.

That's what lawyers are for.

I don't want to see you, standing at the bottom of the

steps,
shimmering into orgasm.
You know how green mammals are;
you're one of them.

Sincerely,

Janet Thalia

In My Next Life

I will not marry
but will stitch hearts to sleeves
and other easily attached
places.

In my next life
I won't try so hard
to make things right
but will just let them be
and that will be
enough.

In my next life
I won't be so mean
Hell will fever the mean out of me.
I will sweat envy
out
my pores
and be no longer distended with pride;
sickness will sweep sloth from my lungs
and wipe lust from my loins.

Only balance will capture
my interest. It will be
the one still
point.